Table of Contents

- Chapter 1: Introduction to Artificial Intelligence 3
  - What is Artificial Intelligence? 3
  - History of AI 3
  - Importance of AI in Today's World 4
- Chapter 2: Basic Concepts of Artificial Intelligence 4
  - Machine Learning 4
  - Neural Networks 5
  - Natural Language Processing 5
- Chapter 3: AI Algorithms and Techniques 6
  - Supervised Learning 6
  - Unsupervised Learning 7
  - Reinforcement Learning 7
- Chapter 4: AI Applications in Various Industries 8
  - Healthcare 8
  - Finance 8
  - Transportation 9
- Chapter 5: Ethical Considerations in Artificial Intelligence 9
  - Bias in AI 9
  - Privacy Concerns 10
  - Job Displacement 11
- Chapter 6: The Ultimate AI Exam 11
  - Multiple Choice Questions 11
  - True or False Questions 12
  - Fill in the Blank Questions 13
- Chapter 7: Answers and Explanations 13
  - Answer Key for Multiple Choice Questions 13
  - Explanation for True or False Questions 14
  - Solutions for Fill in the Blank Questions 14
- Chapter 8: Conclusion 15

    Reflecting on Your AI Knowledge 15
    Next Steps in Your AI Journey 16
100 Test Questions and Answers 17
    Techniques and Algorithms 17
    Applications 17
    Tools and Frameworks 18
    Ethical Considerations 18
    Advanced Concepts 19
    Data and Preprocessing 19
    Performance Evaluation 20
    Specialized AI Topics 20
    AI in Practice 21
    Future Trends and Challenges 21
    AI in Healthcare 22
    AI in Finance 22
    AI in Education 23
    AI in Transportation 23
    AI in Manufacturing 24
    AI in Retail 24
    AI in Entertainment 25
    AI in Cybersecurity 25
    AI in Agriculture 26

Chapter 1: Introduction to Artificial Intelligence

What is Artificial Intelligence?

Artificial Intelligence, often abbreviated as AI, is a branch of computer science that aims to create machines that can perform tasks that typically require human intelligence. These tasks can range from simple actions like recognizing speech or images to more complex activities like driving a car or playing chess. AI systems are designed to learn from data, adapt to new situations, and make decisions without human intervention.

One of the key concepts in AI is machine learning, which involves training algorithms to recognize patterns in data and make predictions based on that information. This process is often done through the use of neural networks, which are algorithms inspired by the structure of the human brain. By feeding large amounts of data into these networks, they can learn to recognize patterns and make decisions with a high degree of accuracy.

Another important concept in AI is natural language processing, which involves the ability of machines to understand and generate human language. This technology is used in applications like virtual assistants, chatbots, and language translation services. By using advanced algorithms and machine learning techniques, AI systems can analyze text, speech, and other forms of communication to extract meaning and respond appropriately.

In recent years, AI has made significant advances in areas like computer vision, speech recognition, and autonomous vehicles. These advancements have led to the development of technologies like self-driving cars, facial recognition systems, and personalized recommendation engines. As AI continues to evolve, it is expected to have a profound impact on industries ranging from healthcare and finance to transportation and entertainment.

In conclusion, Artificial Intelligence is a rapidly growing field that is revolutionizing the way we interact with technology. By understanding the basic concepts of AI, individuals can better appreciate the potential applications and implications of this powerful technology. The Ultimate AI Exam provides a comprehensive overview of AI concepts, along with challenging questions and answers to test your knowledge and deepen your understanding of this exciting field.

History of AI

The history of artificial intelligence (AI) is a fascinating journey that spans several decades. The concept of AI can be traced back to the 1950s when computer scientists began exploring ways to create machines that could mimic human intelligence. One of the earliest breakthroughs in AI came in 1956 when a group of researchers organized the Dartmouth Conference, which is now considered the birthplace of AI.

In the following years, AI research gained momentum as scientists and engineers developed new algorithms and technologies to advance the field. One of the key milestones in the history of AI was the creation of the first neural network in 1958 by Frank Rosenblatt. This groundbreaking development paved the way for machine learning and deep learning, which are now essential components of modern AI systems.

Throughout the 1960s and 1970s, AI research continued to evolve, with researchers focusing on areas such as natural language processing, computer vision, and robotics. In 1973, the development of the first expert system, known as MYCIN, demonstrated the potential of AI in solving complex problems in specific domains. This marked a significant advancement in the field and laid the foundation for future applications of AI in various industries.

The 1980s and 1990s saw a surge in interest and investment in AI, leading to the development of new technologies such as genetic algorithms, fuzzy logic, and reinforcement learning. These advancements enabled AI systems to perform tasks that were previously thought to be beyond the capabilities of machines. The development of IBM's Deep Blue in 1997, which defeated world chess champion Garry Kasparov, showcased the power of AI in solving complex strategic problems.

In the 21st century, AI has become increasingly integrated into our daily lives, with applications ranging from virtual assistants and self-driving cars to healthcare and finance. The rapid advancements in AI technology have raised questions about its impact on society, ethics, and the future of work. As we look to the future, it is essential for individuals to have a solid understanding of AI principles and technologies to navigate the increasingly AI-driven world.

Importance of AI in Today's World

Artificial Intelligence (AI) has become an integral part of today's world, revolutionizing industries and transforming the way we live and work. From self-driving cars to personalized recommendations on streaming platforms, AI is everywhere. Understanding the importance of AI in today's world is crucial for anyone looking to stay ahead in this rapidly evolving landscape.

One of the key reasons why AI is so important today is its ability to automate tasks and processes, increasing efficiency and productivity. Businesses are increasingly turning to AI-powered solutions to streamline operations and reduce costs. For individuals looking to test their AI knowledge, understanding how AI can improve workflows and optimize performance is essential to success in the field.

AI also plays a crucial role in decision-making processes, providing valuable insights and predictions based on data analysis. From predicting customer behavior to optimizing supply chains, AI algorithms are helping businesses make informed decisions faster and more accurately than ever before. Testing your knowledge of AI in this context can help you understand how to leverage AI for strategic decision-making in various industries.

In addition to automation and decision-making, AI is also driving innovation and creativity in various fields. From healthcare to finance, AI is enabling breakthroughs in research and development, pushing the boundaries of what is possible. For individuals seeking to test their AI knowledge, exploring the ways in which AI is fueling innovation and creating new opportunities can provide valuable insights into the future of technology.

Overall, the importance of AI in today's world cannot be overstated. As AI continues to advance and reshape industries, understanding its capabilities and implications is crucial for anyone looking to navigate this rapidly changing landscape. Testing your knowledge of AI through questions and answers can help you stay informed and prepared for the challenges and opportunities that lie ahead in the world of artificial intelligence.

Chapter 2: Basic Concepts of Artificial Intelligence

Machine Learning

Machine learning is a crucial component of artificial intelligence, allowing machines to learn from data and improve their performance without being explicitly programmed. It is a subset of AI that focuses on developing algorithms that can learn from and make predictions or decisions based on data. In the field of machine learning, there are various techniques such as supervised learning, unsupervised learning, and reinforcement learning.

One of the most common types of machine learning is supervised learning, where the algorithm is trained on labeled data to make predictions. This type of learning is widely used in applications such as image recognition, speech recognition, and natural language processing. Unsupervised learning, on the other hand, involves training the algorithm on unlabeled data to identify patterns or relationships within the data.

Reinforcement learning is another important aspect of machine learning, where the algorithm learns to make decisions by interacting with an environment and receiving feedback in the form of rewards or penalties. This type of learning is often used in robotics, gaming, and autonomous vehicles. Overall, machine learning plays a crucial role in enabling machines to perform tasks that were once thought to be exclusive to human intelligence.

To test your knowledge of machine learning, it is essential to understand the various algorithms and techniques used in this field. Questions may include identifying the difference between supervised and unsupervised learning, explaining how reinforcement learning works, or applying machine learning concepts to real-world scenarios. By testing your knowledge of machine learning, you can assess your understanding of this fundamental aspect of artificial intelligence and identify areas for further study and improvement. So, are you ready to put your machine learning knowledge to the test?

Neural Networks

Neural networks are a crucial component of artificial intelligence (AI) technology. These networks are designed to mimic the way the human brain operates, with layers of interconnected nodes that process information and make decisions based on that data. Understanding how neural networks work is essential for anyone looking to test their knowledge of AI.

One key concept to grasp when it comes to neural networks is the idea of layers. Neural networks are typically made up of multiple layers, each with its own set of nodes. The input layer receives data, the hidden layers process that data, and the output layer produces the final result. This layered approach allows neural networks to handle complex tasks and make complex decisions.

Another important aspect of neural networks is the concept of training. Before a neural network can be used effectively, it must be trained on a dataset. During training, the network adjusts its connections and weights to minimize errors and improve accuracy. This process is essential for ensuring that the neural network can perform its intended tasks accurately.

There are several different types of neural networks, each suited to different types of tasks. For example, convolutional neural networks are commonly used for image recognition, while recurrent neural networks are often used for natural language processing. Understanding the strengths and weaknesses of each type of neural network is crucial for anyone looking to test their AI knowledge.

In conclusion, neural networks are a fundamental aspect of artificial intelligence technology. By understanding how neural networks work, including their layers, training process, and different types, individuals can better test their knowledge of AI. Whether you're preparing for an AI exam or simply looking to expand your understanding of this cutting-edge technology, neural networks are a topic worth exploring.

Natural Language Processing

Natural Language Processing (NLP) is a subfield of artificial intelligence that focuses on the interaction between computers and human language. It is a crucial component of many AI systems, enabling machines to understand, interpret, and generate human language. NLP has a wide range of applications, from chatbots and virtual assistants to language translation and sentiment analysis.

One of the key challenges in NLP is the ambiguity and complexity of human language. Words and phrases can have multiple meanings, and context plays a crucial role in determining the correct interpretation. NLP algorithms must be able to handle this ambiguity and infer the correct meaning based on the context in which the language is used.

There are several techniques used in NLP, including natural language understanding (NLU) and natural language generation (NLG). NLU involves extracting meaning from text, while NLG involves generating human-like language from data. These techniques are often used in combination to create more sophisticated NLP systems.

NLP is constantly evolving, with new techniques and algorithms being developed to improve the accuracy and performance of AI systems. As the field continues to advance, it is important for individuals interested in AI to stay up-to-date on the latest developments in NLP. By testing your knowledge of NLP through questions and answers, you can assess your understanding of this important subfield of AI and identify areas where you may need to further your knowledge.

Chapter 3: AI Algorithms and Techniques

Supervised Learning

Supervised learning is a fundamental concept in the field of artificial intelligence (AI) that involves training a model on a labeled dataset to make predictions or decisions. In supervised learning, the algorithm learns to map input data to output labels based on examples provided in the training data. This type of learning is used in a wide range of applications, including image recognition, speech recognition, and natural language processing.

One of the key advantages of supervised learning is that it allows for the creation of accurate predictive models. By providing the algorithm with labeled training data, it can learn to make predictions on new, unseen data with a high degree of accuracy. This is particularly useful in situations where there is a large amount of data available, such as in medical diagnosis or financial forecasting.

To test your knowledge of supervised learning, consider the following question: What is the difference between classification and regression in supervised learning? Classification involves predicting discrete labels or categories, such as whether an email is spam or not spam. Regression, on the other hand, involves predicting continuous values, such as the price of a house based on its features. Understanding the difference between these two types of supervised learning tasks is essential for building effective AI models.

Another important concept in supervised learning is the notion of overfitting. Overfitting occurs when a model learns the training data too well, to the point where it performs poorly on new, unseen data. This can happen if the model is too complex or if there is noise in the training data. To prevent overfitting, techniques such as cross-validation and regularization can be used to ensure that the model generalizes well to new data.

In summary, supervised learning is a powerful tool in the field of artificial intelligence that allows for the creation of accurate predictive models. By training algorithms on labeled data, it is possible to make predictions on new, unseen data with a high degree of accuracy. Understanding key concepts such as classification, regression, and overfitting is essential for anyone looking to test their knowledge of AI and machine learning.

Unsupervised Learning

Unsupervised learning is a type of machine learning that involves training algorithms on data without labels or guidance. This means that the algorithm must find patterns and relationships within the data on its own, without any external assistance. Unsupervised learning is particularly useful for tasks such as clustering, anomaly detection, and dimensionality reduction.

One common technique used in unsupervised learning is clustering, which involves grouping similar data points together based on their characteristics. This can help identify patterns and structures within the data that may not be immediately obvious. Another technique is anomaly detection, which involves identifying outliers or unusual data points that do not fit the overall pattern of the data set.

Dimensionality reduction is another important application of unsupervised learning, which involves reducing the number of features or variables in a data set while still preserving as much information as possible. This can help simplify the data and make it easier to analyze and interpret.

Overall, unsupervised learning plays a crucial role in the field of artificial intelligence by allowing algorithms to learn from data without explicit guidance. By testing your knowledge of unsupervised learning, you can gain a better understanding of how AI algorithms work and how they can be applied to real-world problems. So, are you ready to put your AI knowledge to the test with questions and answers on unsupervised learning?

Reinforcement Learning

Reinforcement learning is a key concept in artificial intelligence that focuses on teaching machines to make decisions based on trial and error. In this subchapter, we will explore the fundamentals of reinforcement learning and how it is applied in the field of AI. By understanding the principles of reinforcement learning, you can test your knowledge and deepen your understanding of this important aspect of artificial intelligence.

One of the key components of reinforcement learning is the concept of rewards and penalties. When a machine takes an action, it receives either a positive reward or a negative penalty based on the outcome of that action. This feedback loop helps the machine learn which actions lead to positive outcomes and which ones should be avoided. By understanding how rewards and penalties shape the behavior of machines, you can better grasp the mechanics of reinforcement learning.

Another important aspect of reinforcement learning is the idea of exploration and exploitation. Machines must strike a balance between trying new actions to discover better strategies (exploration) and exploiting known strategies to maximize rewards (exploitation). Finding the optimal balance between exploration and exploitation is a key challenge in reinforcement learning, and mastering this concept is essential for anyone seeking to test their AI knowledge.

Reinforcement learning algorithms are often used in applications such as game playing and robotics. By training machines to make decisions based on rewards and penalties, researchers have been able to develop AI systems that can outperform humans in complex games like chess and Go. Understanding how reinforcement learning algorithms are applied in real-world scenarios can provide valuable insights into the capabilities of artificial intelligence.

In conclusion, reinforcement learning is a fundamental concept in artificial intelligence that involves teaching machines to make decisions based on trial and error. By understanding the principles of rewards and penalties, exploration and exploitation, and real-world applications of reinforcement learning algorithms, you can deepen your knowledge of AI and test your understanding of this important field. Whether you are a novice looking to learn more about AI or an expert seeking to test your knowledge, mastering the principles of reinforcement learning is essential for anyone interested in the field of artificial intelligence.

Chapter 4: AI Applications in Various Industries

Healthcare

Healthcare is one of the many industries that has seen significant advancements with the integration of artificial intelligence (AI) technology. From improving patient care to streamlining administrative tasks, AI has revolutionized the way healthcare professionals work. In this subchapter, we will explore some of the key ways in which AI is transforming the healthcare industry and how it is being used to improve patient outcomes.

One of the most significant applications of AI in healthcare is in medical imaging. AI algorithms have been developed to analyze medical images, such as X-rays, MRIs, and CT scans, to help diagnose diseases and conditions more accurately and quickly. These algorithms can detect patterns and abnormalities that may be missed by human radiologists, leading to earlier detection and treatment of diseases.

Another important use of AI in healthcare is in personalized medicine. By analyzing large amounts of patient data, AI can help healthcare providers tailor treatment plans to individual patients based on their genetic makeup, lifestyle, and other factors. This personalized approach can lead to more effective treatments and better outcomes for patients.

AI is also being used to improve the efficiency of healthcare systems. By automating routine tasks, such as scheduling appointments, processing insurance claims, and managing medical records, AI can help healthcare providers save time and resources, allowing them to focus more on patient care. This can lead to shorter wait times, reduced administrative costs, and improved overall patient satisfaction.

In addition to these applications, AI is also being used to predict and prevent diseases. By analyzing data from electronic health records, wearable devices, and other sources, AI can identify patterns and trends that may indicate a potential health problem. This early detection can help healthcare providers intervene sooner and take preventive measures to reduce the risk of developing a serious illness.

Overall, the integration of AI technology in healthcare has the potential to revolutionize the industry and improve patient outcomes. By harnessing the power of AI to analyze data, automate tasks, and personalize treatments, healthcare professionals can provide more efficient and effective care to their patients. As AI continues to advance, the possibilities for its applications in healthcare are virtually limitless, making it an exciting time to be involved in this rapidly evolving field.

Finance

In the world of artificial intelligence, understanding finance is crucial for success. Finance plays a major role in the development and implementation of AI technologies, as it determines how resources are allocated and managed. In this subchapter, we will explore the intersection of finance and AI, and how they work together to drive innovation and growth.

One of the key areas where AI is making a significant impact in finance is in the realm of predictive analytics. AI algorithms are being used to analyze vast amounts of financial data in real-time, allowing companies to make more informed decisions and predict future trends. This has revolutionized the way financial institutions operate, enabling them to better manage risk, identify opportunities, and optimize their operations.

Another important application of AI in finance is in the realm of algorithmic trading. AI-powered trading systems can analyze market data and execute trades at lightning speed, far faster and more accurately than any human trader could. This has led to a rise in the use of AI-driven trading strategies, which have the potential to deliver higher returns and reduce risk for investors.

In addition to predictive analytics and algorithmic trading, AI is also being used in finance for fraud detection and prevention. By analyzing patterns and anomalies in financial transactions, AI algorithms can flag potentially fraudulent activity in real-time, helping to protect companies and consumers from financial losses. This has become increasingly important in today's digital economy, where cyber threats are on the rise.

Overall, the integration of AI and finance is transforming the industry in profound ways. As AI technologies continue to advance, they will play an increasingly important role in shaping the future of finance. By understanding the intersection of finance and AI, you can stay ahead of the curve and leverage these technologies to drive innovation and success in your own financial endeavors.

Transportation

Transportation is a crucial aspect of artificial intelligence that plays a significant role in various industries. From self-driving cars to drones, AI technology is revolutionizing the way we move from one place to another. In this subchapter, we will explore the different ways AI is transforming the transportation sector and how it is impacting our daily lives.

One of the most prominent examples of AI in transportation is the development of autonomous vehicles. These vehicles use AI algorithms to navigate roads, make decisions, and avoid obstacles without human intervention. Companies like Tesla, Google, and Uber are leading the way in developing self-driving cars that are set to revolutionize the way we commute in the future.

Another area where AI is making a significant impact is in traffic management and optimization. AI algorithms can analyze vast amounts of data in real-time to predict traffic patterns, optimize traffic flow, and reduce congestion on roads. This not only saves time for commuters but also reduces carbon emissions and makes transportation more efficient.

In addition to self-driving cars and traffic management, AI is also being used in the development of drone technology. Drones equipped with AI can be used for various purposes, such as delivery services, surveillance, and search and rescue operations. These unmanned aerial vehicles are changing the way we think about transportation and opening up new possibilities for industries like logistics and emergency response.

Overall, the integration of AI technology in transportation is transforming the way we move goods and people from one place to another. As the technology continues to advance, we can expect to see even more innovative solutions that will make transportation safer, more efficient, and more sustainable. So, if you want to test your AI knowledge in transportation, be prepared to learn about the latest developments and advancements in this exciting field.

Chapter 5: Ethical Considerations in Artificial Intelligence

Bias in AI

Bias in AI is a crucial topic that every individual interested in artificial intelligence should be aware of. Bias in AI refers to the unfair or unjust prejudices that can be embedded into machine learning algorithms due to the data used to train them. This bias can lead to discriminatory outcomes, perpetuating inequalities in society. It is essential for those taking an AI exam to understand how bias can influence the performance of AI systems and how to mitigate it.

One common source of bias in AI is biased data. If the data used to train an AI model is not representative of the diverse populations it will interact with, the model may produce biased results. For example, if a facial recognition system is trained primarily on data from one demographic group, it may perform poorly when trying to recognize faces from other groups. To address this, it is important to ensure that the training data is diverse and balanced to avoid bias in AI systems.

Another source of bias in AI is the design of the algorithm itself. If the algorithm contains inherent biases or assumptions, these biases can be amplified when applied to real-world scenarios. For example, a predictive policing algorithm that relies on historical crime data may perpetuate racial biases if the data used to train it is biased. It is crucial for those studying for an AI exam to understand how the design of algorithms can influence bias and how to create more fair and transparent AI systems.

To mitigate bias in AI, researchers and practitioners can employ techniques such as fairness-aware machine learning, bias detection algorithms, and diverse data sampling. Fairness-aware machine learning involves incorporating fairness constraints into the training process to ensure that the AI model does not produce discriminatory outcomes. Bias detection algorithms can help identify biases in AI systems, allowing researchers to address them before deployment. Additionally, using diverse data sampling techniques can help reduce bias by ensuring that the training data is representative of the populations the AI system will interact with.

In conclusion, bias in AI is a critical issue that must be addressed by those studying artificial intelligence. Understanding how bias can impact AI systems and learning how to mitigate it is essential for creating fair and ethical AI technologies. By being aware of the sources of bias in AI, such as biased data and algorithm design, and employing mitigation techniques, individuals can help create more inclusive and equitable AI systems. Test your knowledge of bias in AI by exploring questions and answers related to this topic in the Ultimate AI Exam.

Privacy Concerns

Privacy concerns are a crucial aspect to consider when dealing with artificial intelligence (AI) technology. As AI continues to advance and become more integrated into our daily lives, the issue of privacy becomes increasingly important. Individuals are rightfully concerned about how their personal information is being used and shared by AI systems.

One major privacy concern with AI is the collection and storage of personal data. AI systems often rely on large amounts of data to function effectively, which can include sensitive information such as financial records, health data, and even personal communications. This raises questions about who has access to this data and how it is being used. There is a risk that personal information could be misused or leaked, leading to potential privacy breaches.

Another privacy concern is the lack of transparency in AI algorithms. Many AI systems operate using complex algorithms that are difficult for the average person to understand. This lack of transparency can make it challenging to know how decisions are being made and what data is being used to inform those decisions. This can lead to concerns about bias, discrimination, and other ethical issues in AI systems.

Furthermore, there is a growing concern about the potential for AI systems to infringe on individual privacy rights. As AI technology becomes more advanced, there is a risk that it could be used to monitor and track individuals without their knowledge or consent. This raises questions about the boundaries of surveillance and the need for strong privacy protections to safeguard individual rights.

In conclusion, privacy concerns are a critical issue to consider when it comes to AI technology. As AI continues to advance, it is important for individuals to be aware of the potential risks and to advocate for strong privacy protections. By understanding the risks and advocating for transparency and accountability in AI systems, we can help ensure that personal privacy rights are protected in the age of artificial intelligence.

Job Displacement

Job displacement is a growing concern in the age of artificial intelligence (AI). As AI technology continues to advance, more and more tasks traditionally performed by humans are being automated. This has led to a shift in the labor market, with certain jobs becoming obsolete and new roles emerging that require a different skill set. For a person that wants to test their AI knowledge with a test, understanding the impact of job displacement is crucial.

One of the main reasons for job displacement is the ability of AI systems to perform tasks more efficiently and accurately than humans. This has led to the automation of repetitive and routine tasks in industries such as manufacturing, customer service, and transportation. As a result, many workers in these sectors are at risk of being displaced by AI technology. It is important for individuals to stay informed about the latest developments in AI and how they may affect their job prospects.

In addition to job displacement, AI technology also has the potential to create new job opportunities. As AI systems become more sophisticated, there is a growing demand for professionals with expertise in areas such as machine learning, data analysis, and programming. For individuals looking to test their AI knowledge with a test, it is important to stay up-to-date on the skills and competencies that are in demand in the AI job market.

To prepare for the impact of job displacement caused by AI technology, individuals can take proactive steps to enhance their skills and adapt to the changing labor market. This may involve pursuing additional education and training in AI-related fields, such as computer science, data science, or robotics. By staying ahead of the curve and acquiring new skills, individuals can position themselves for success in an AI-driven economy.

In conclusion, job displacement is a significant issue in the age of artificial intelligence. For individuals looking to test their AI knowledge with a test, understanding the implications of AI technology on the labor market is essential. By staying informed about the latest developments in AI, acquiring new skills, and adapting to the changing job market, individuals can navigate the challenges of job displacement and thrive in an AI-driven economy.

Chapter 6: The Ultimate AI Exam

Multiple Choice Questions

Are you ready to put your AI knowledge to the test? In this subchapter, we will explore a series of multiple choice questions that will challenge your understanding of artificial intelligence concepts. By answering these questions, you will not only assess your current knowledge but also gain valuable insights into the world of AI.

Question 1: What is the primary goal of artificial intelligence?
A) To replace human intelligence
B) To mimic human intelligence
C) To enhance human intelligence
D) To control human intelligence

Question 2: Which of the following is an example of supervised learning in AI?
A) Image recognition
B) Speech recognition
C) Reinforcement learning
D) Natural language processing

Question 3: What is the role of neural networks in artificial intelligence?
A) To store and retrieve information
B) To process and analyze data
C) To generate random outputs
D) To predict future trends

Question 4: Which programming language is commonly used in developing AI applications?
A) Java
B) Python
C) C++
D) Ruby

Question 5: What is the significance of the Turing Test in the field of artificial intelligence?
A) It measures a machine's ability to exhibit intelligent behavior
B) It determines a machine's processing speed
C) It evaluates a machine's memory capacity
D) It tests a machine's physical dexterity

By answering these multiple choice questions, you will gain a deeper understanding of artificial intelligence concepts and principles. Test your knowledge today and see how well you fare in the world of AI. Good luck!

True or False Questions

Welcome to the subchapter on "True or False Questions" from "The Ultimate AI Exam: Test Your Knowledge with Questions and Answers." This section is designed specifically for individuals who want to test their AI knowledge with a series of true or false questions. This is a great way to challenge yourself and see how well you understand the concepts and principles of artificial intelligence.

In this section, you will find a variety of true or false questions that cover a range of topics related to AI. These questions are designed to test your understanding of key concepts such as machine learning, neural networks, natural language processing, and more. By answering these questions, you will be able to gauge your knowledge and identify areas where you may need to further study or review.

As you work through the true or false questions in this section, be sure to take your time and carefully consider each statement before selecting your answer. It can be easy to rush through the questions, but by taking your time and thinking critically about each statement, you will be able to more accurately assess your understanding of AI concepts.

After you have completed the true or false questions in this section, be sure to review the answers to see how well you did. This will give you valuable feedback on your knowledge of AI and help you identify any areas where you may need to focus your study efforts. Remember, the goal of this exam is to challenge yourself and improve your understanding of artificial intelligence, so don't be discouraged if you don't get every question right. Use this as an opportunity to learn and grow in your knowledge of AI. Good luck!

Fill in the Blank Questions

Fill in the blank questions are a common type of assessment used to test knowledge and understanding of a particular subject. In the context of AI exams, fill in the blank questions can be a valuable tool for evaluating a person's understanding of key concepts and principles in artificial intelligence. These questions typically require the test-taker to provide a specific word or phrase that completes a sentence or statement.

For a person that wants to test their AI knowledge with a test, fill in the blank questions can be a great way to assess their understanding of key AI concepts. These questions can cover a range of topics, from basic definitions and principles to more advanced theories and applications of artificial intelligence. By providing a blank space for the test-taker to fill in, these questions require them to actively recall and apply their knowledge of AI concepts.

In the Ultimate AI Exam: Test Your Knowledge with Questions and Answers, fill in the blank questions are included to challenge and engage test-takers in their AI knowledge. These questions are carefully crafted to cover a wide range of AI topics, ensuring that test-takers have a comprehensive understanding of artificial intelligence. By including fill in the blank questions, the exam aims to test not only the test-taker's ability to recall information, but also their ability to apply that knowledge in a meaningful way.

To excel in answering fill in the blank questions in an AI exam, test-takers should review key AI concepts and principles before the exam. This will help ensure that they have a solid understanding of the material and can confidently fill in the blanks with the correct answers. Additionally, practicing with sample fill in the blank questions can help test-takers become familiar with the format and structure of these questions, allowing them to approach them more effectively during the exam.

Overall, fill in the blank questions are an important component of any AI exam, as they require test-takers to actively engage with the material and demonstrate their understanding of key AI concepts. By including these questions in the Ultimate AI Exam, test-takers can test their knowledge of artificial intelligence in a challenging and interactive way. So, if you're looking to test your AI knowledge, be prepared to tackle some fill in the blank questions in the Ultimate AI Exam!

Chapter 7: Answers and Explanations

Answer Key for Multiple Choice Questions

In this subchapter, you will find the answer key for the multiple choice questions that were included in the previous chapter. This will allow you to check your answers and see how well you did on the AI exam. Make sure to compare your responses to the correct answers provided here to gauge your understanding of the material.

Question 1: What is the primary goal of artificial intelligence?
Answer: b) To create machines that can perform tasks that typically require human intelligence

Question 2: Which of the following is an example of artificial narrow intelligence (ANI)?
Answer: a) Siri, Apple's virtual assistant

Question 3: What is the Turing Test?
Answer: c) A test of a machine's ability to exhibit intelligent behavior equivalent to, or indistinguishable from, that of a human

Question 4: What is machine learning?
Answer: d) A subset of AI that allows machines to learn from data and improve over time without being explicitly programmed

Question 5: What is the difference between supervised and unsupervised learning?
Answer: a) Supervised learning requires labeled data for training, while unsupervised learning does not require labeled data

By reviewing the answers provided here, you can assess your knowledge of artificial intelligence concepts and see where you may need to focus your studies further. Remember, practice makes perfect when it comes to mastering AI concepts, so keep testing yourself with questions like these to improve your understanding.

Explanation for True or False Questions

In this subchapter, we will delve into the nuances of true or false questions in the context of AI exams. True or false questions are a common format used in assessments to test the knowledge and understanding of test-takers. These questions present a statement, and the test-taker must determine whether the statement is true or false based on their understanding of the subject matter.

When tackling true or false questions in an AI exam, it is crucial to carefully read each statement and consider the information provided. It is important to remember that even if part of a statement is true, if any part is false, the entire statement should be marked as false. This requires a keen eye for detail and a solid understanding of the concepts being tested.

One key strategy for approaching true or false questions is to avoid making assumptions or jumping to conclusions. Each statement should be evaluated based on the information provided in the question and any relevant knowledge you possess. It can be helpful to underline key terms or phrases in the statement to ensure you are focusing on the most important details.

Another important aspect to keep in mind when answering true or false questions is to avoid second-guessing yourself. If you are confident in your answer based on the information presented, trust your instincts and move on to the next question. Overthinking can lead to unnecessary confusion and potentially incorrect answers.

In conclusion, true or false questions can be a valuable tool for testing your AI knowledge in an exam setting. By approaching these questions with a clear understanding of the concepts being tested, attention to detail, and confidence in your answers, you can effectively demonstrate your knowledge and skills in the field of artificial intelligence. Remember to stay focused, trust your instincts, and approach each question with a strategic mindset to maximize your chances of success on the exam.

Solutions for Fill in the Blank Questions

For those looking to test their knowledge of artificial intelligence, fill in the blank questions can be a great way to challenge yourself and see how much you really know. However, these types of questions can also be tricky if you're not sure where to start. In this subchapter, we will explore some solutions for fill in the blank questions to help you sharpen your AI skills and ace your next exam.

One of the best strategies for tackling fill in the blank questions is to carefully read the entire question before attempting to fill in the blank. This will give you a better understanding of what the question is asking and help you identify any key terms or concepts that may be missing. Once you have a clear grasp of the question, you can then use your knowledge of AI principles to fill in the blank with the correct answer.

Another helpful tip for solving fill in the blank questions is to look for clues within the question itself. Sometimes, the wording or structure of the question can provide hints about what the missing word or phrase should be. For example, if the question is asking about a specific AI algorithm or programming language, you can use your knowledge of these topics to narrow down your options and make an educated guess.

If you're still unsure about how to approach a fill in the blank question, don't be afraid to use the process of elimination. By ruling out incorrect answers or options that don't make sense in the context of the question, you can increase your chances of selecting the correct answer. This method can be especially useful when you're faced with multiple choice fill in the blank questions that offer several possible solutions.

Lastly, practice makes perfect when it comes to mastering fill in the blank questions on AI exams. The more you familiarize yourself with different AI concepts, algorithms, and techniques, the more confident you'll become in your ability to answer fill in the blank questions accurately. Consider using study guides, practice exams, or online resources to hone your skills and prepare yourself for any fill in the blank questions that may come your way. By following these strategies and tips, you can boost your confidence and improve your performance on AI exams.

Chapter 8: Conclusion

Reflecting on Your AI Knowledge

Now that you have completed the AI exam and answered all the questions, it's time to reflect on your knowledge of artificial intelligence. This subchapter will guide you through analyzing your performance and understanding where you stand in terms of AI expertise.

First and foremost, consider the questions you found easy and those that were challenging for you. Did you excel in certain topics, such as machine learning or natural language processing, or did you struggle to grasp concepts like neural networks or deep learning? Identifying your strengths and weaknesses will help you focus on areas that need improvement.

Next, think about how you approached the questions during the exam. Did you rely on memorization or did you apply critical thinking skills to analyze and solve problems? Understanding your test-taking strategies can provide insight into your overall understanding of AI concepts and algorithms.

Furthermore, consider seeking feedback from a mentor, peer, or AI expert to gain an outside perspective on your performance. They may offer valuable insights and suggestions for further study or practice to enhance your AI knowledge and skills.

Finally, use your exam results as a learning opportunity to set goals for future growth and development in the field of artificial intelligence. Whether you aim to pursue a career in AI or simply have a passion for the subject, reflecting on your performance will help you continue on your journey to becoming an AI expert. Remember, learning is a continuous process, and there is always room for improvement and advancement in the exciting world of artificial intelligence.

Next Steps in Your AI Journey

Congratulations on completing this AI exam and testing your knowledge in the field of artificial intelligence! This subchapter, "Next Steps in Your AI Journey," is designed to provide you with guidance on what to do next in your pursuit of furthering your understanding of AI. Whether you aced the exam or found areas that need improvement, there are always opportunities for growth and learning in this rapidly evolving field.

One of the first steps you may want to consider is diving deeper into specific areas of AI that you found particularly challenging or intriguing during the exam. This could involve taking online courses, attending workshops or conferences, or reading books and research papers on the subject. By honing in on your weaknesses or interests, you can gain a more comprehensive understanding of AI and expand your knowledge base.

Another important next step in your AI journey is to start applying what you have learned in practical ways. This could involve working on AI projects, collaborating with others in the field, or even pursuing internships or job opportunities in AI-related industries. By gaining hands-on experience, you can solidify your understanding of AI concepts and techniques and see how they are applied in real-world scenarios.

Networking with other professionals in the AI field can also be a valuable next step in your journey. By connecting with experts, researchers, and practitioners in the industry, you can gain valuable insights, advice, and mentorship that can help guide you in your AI pursuits. Joining AI communities, attending meetups, and engaging in online forums are great ways to start building your network and tapping into the collective knowledge of the AI community.

Finally, don't forget to continue challenging yourself and testing your AI knowledge regularly. Whether it's taking more exams, participating in AI competitions, or working on personal projects, staying engaged and curious about AI will help you stay ahead of the curve and continue growing in your understanding of this fascinating field. Remember, the journey to mastering AI is a lifelong pursuit, so embrace the challenges and opportunities that come your way as you continue to expand your knowledge and skills in artificial intelligence.

100 Test Questions and Answers

1. **Q:** What is Artificial Intelligence (AI)? **A:** AI is the simulation of human intelligence in machines that are programmed to think and learn like humans.
2. **Q:** What are the main types of AI? **A:** The main types are Narrow AI, General AI, and Superintelligent AI.
3. **Q:** What is Machine Learning (ML)? **A:** ML is a subset of AI that focuses on building systems that can learn from and make decisions based on data.
4. **Q:** What is a neural network? **A:** A neural network is a series of algorithms that attempt to recognize underlying relationships in a set of data through a process that mimics the way the human brain operates.
5. **Q:** What is deep learning? **A:** Deep learning is a subset of machine learning involving neural networks with many layers, often referred to as deep neural networks.

Techniques and Algorithms

6. **Q:** What is supervised learning? **A:** Supervised learning is a type of ML where the model is trained on labeled data.
7. **Q:** What is unsupervised learning? **A:** Unsupervised learning is a type of ML where the model is trained on unlabeled data.
8. **Q:** What is reinforcement learning? **A:** Reinforcement learning is a type of ML where an agent learns to make decisions by performing actions and receiving rewards or penalties.
9. **Q:** What is a decision tree? **A:** A decision tree is a flowchart-like structure used for classification and regression tasks, where each node represents a decision point.
10. **Q:** What is overfitting in machine learning? **A:** Overfitting occurs when a model learns the training data too well, capturing noise and details that do not generalize to new data.

Applications

11. **Q:** Name some applications of AI. **A:** Applications include natural language processing, image recognition, autonomous vehicles, and recommendation systems.
12. **Q:** What is natural language processing (NLP)? **A:** NLP is a field of AI focused on the interaction between computers and humans through natural language.

13. **Q:** What is a chatbot? **A:** A chatbot is an AI application that can simulate a conversation with a user in natural language.
14. **Q:** What is computer vision? **A:** Computer vision is a field of AI that trains computers to interpret and make decisions based on visual data.
15. **Q:** What is a recommendation system? **A:** A recommendation system is an AI system that provides users with personalized content or product suggestions based on their preferences and behavior.

Tools and Frameworks

16. **Q:** Name some popular machine learning frameworks. **A:** Popular frameworks include TensorFlow, PyTorch, scikit-learn, and Keras.
17. **Q:** What is TensorFlow? **A:** TensorFlow is an open-source machine learning framework developed by Google for building and training neural networks.
18. **Q:** What is PyTorch? **A:** PyTorch is an open-source machine learning library developed by Facebook's AI Research lab, known for its flexibility and dynamic computation graph.
19. **Q:** What is scikit-learn? **A:** Scikit-learn is an open-source machine learning library for Python, offering simple and efficient tools for data mining and data analysis.
20. **Q:** What is Keras? **A:** Keras is an open-source software library that provides a Python interface for neural networks, capable of running on top of TensorFlow or Theano.

Ethical Considerations

21. **Q:** What are some ethical concerns related to AI? **A:** Ethical concerns include bias in algorithms, privacy issues, job displacement, and the potential for misuse.
22. **Q:** What is AI bias? **A:** AI bias occurs when an AI system produces results that are systematically prejudiced due to erroneous assumptions in the machine learning process.
23. **Q:** What is explainable AI (XAI)? **A:** XAI refers to AI systems that are designed to be transparent and understandable by humans, making their decision-making processes clear.
24. **Q:** Why is data privacy important in AI? **A:** Data privacy is crucial because AI systems often require large amounts of data, and mishandling this data can lead to breaches of privacy and misuse of personal information.

25. **Q:** How can AI be used responsibly? **A:** AI can be used responsibly by ensuring transparency, addressing bias, respecting privacy, and considering the social impact of AI applications.

Advanced Concepts

26. **Q:** What is a convolutional neural network (CNN)? **A:** A CNN is a type of neural network particularly well-suited for image recognition and processing, characterized by its use of convolutional layers.
27. **Q:** What is a recurrent neural network (RNN)? **A:** An RNN is a type of neural network designed for sequence data, where connections between nodes form a directed graph along a temporal sequence.
28. **Q:** What is a generative adversarial network (GAN)? **A:** A GAN is a type of neural network where two networks, a generator and a discriminator, are trained simultaneously through adversarial processes.
29. **Q:** What is transfer learning? **A:** Transfer learning is a machine learning technique where a pre-trained model is adapted to a new but related task, improving efficiency and performance.
30. **Q:** What is a support vector machine (SVM)? **A:** An SVM is a supervised learning algorithm used for classification and regression tasks, which works by finding the hyperplane that best separates the data into classes.

Data and Preprocessing

31. **Q:** Why is data preprocessing important in AI? **A:** Data preprocessing is crucial because it cleans and transforms raw data into a suitable format for model training, improving accuracy and efficiency.
32. **Q:** What is feature engineering? **A:** Feature engineering involves creating new features from raw data to improve the performance of machine learning models.
33. **Q:** What is normalization in data preprocessing? **A:** Normalization is the process of scaling data to a standard range, typically between 0 and 1, to ensure that each feature contributes equally to the model.
34. **Q:** What is data augmentation? **A:** Data augmentation is a technique used to increase the amount of training data by generating new data points through transformations like rotation, translation, and flipping.
35. **Q:** What is a confusion matrix? **A:** A confusion matrix is a table used to evaluate the performance of a classification model, showing the actual versus predicted classifications.

Performance Evaluation

36. **Q:** What is precision in the context of machine learning? **A:** Precision is the ratio of correctly predicted positive observations to the total predicted positives, indicating the accuracy of positive predictions.
37. **Q:** What is recall in the context of machine learning? **A:** Recall is the ratio of correctly predicted positive observations to the all observations in actual class, indicating the ability to find all positive samples.
38. **Q:** What is F1 score? **A:** The F1 score is the harmonic mean of precision and recall, providing a single metric that balances both concerns.
39. **Q:** What is cross-validation? **A:** Cross-validation is a technique for assessing how well a model generalizes to an independent dataset by partitioning the data into subsets and training/testing multiple times.
40. **Q:** What is a ROC curve? **A:** A ROC (Receiver Operating Characteristic) curve is a graphical plot illustrating the diagnostic ability of a binary classifier as its discrimination threshold is varied.

Specialized AI Topics

41. **Q:** What is an autoencoder? **A:** An autoencoder is a type of neural network used to learn efficient codings of input data, typically for the purposes of dimensionality reduction or feature learning.
42. **Q:** What is a Boltzmann machine? **A:** A Boltzmann machine is a type of stochastic recurrent neural network capable of learning internal representations.
43. **Q:** What is a Bayesian network? **A:** A Bayesian network is a probabilistic graphical model that represents a set of variables and their conditional dependencies via a directed acyclic graph.
44. **Q:** What is the difference between strong AI and weak AI? **A:** Strong AI, also known as Artificial General Intelligence (AGI), refers to systems that possess the ability to understand, learn, and apply knowledge in a generalized way. Weak AI, or Narrow AI, refers to systems designed for a specific task or narrow range of tasks.
45. **Q:** What is natural language generation (NLG)? **A:** NLG is the process of automatically generating human-like text from structured data, often used in applications like chatbots, report generation, and language translation.

AI in Practice

46. **Q:** What is the Turing Test? **A:** The Turing Test is a measure of a machine's ability to exhibit intelligent behavior indistinguishable from that of a human.
47. **Q:** What is the role of big data in AI? **A:** Big data provides the vast amounts of data necessary to train and improve AI models, enabling more accurate and efficient AI solutions.
48. **Q:** What is edge AI? **A:** Edge AI refers to deploying AI algorithms on devices at the edge of the network, close to the data source, to reduce latency and improve real-time processing.
49. **Q:** What is federated learning? **A:** Federated learning is a technique where multiple decentralized devices collaboratively train a model without sharing raw data, enhancing privacy and security.
50. **Q:** How can AI be integrated into business processes? **A:** AI can be integrated into business processes by automating routine tasks, enhancing decision-making with data-driven insights, personalizing customer experiences, and optimizing operations through predictive analytics.

Future Trends and Challenges

51. **Q:** What is quantum computing's potential impact on AI? **A:** Quantum computing could significantly accelerate AI computations, solving complex problems faster than classical computers, potentially transforming fields like cryptography, optimization, and simulation.
52. **Q:** What is AI democratization? **A:** AI democratization refers to making AI technology accessible to a broader audience, enabling non-experts to use AI tools and systems through user-friendly interfaces and platforms.
53. **Q:** What is the AI alignment problem? **A:** The AI alignment problem involves ensuring that AI systems' goals and behaviors align with human values and intentions, preventing unintended harmful consequences.
54. **Q:** What are AI ethics guidelines? **A:** AI ethics guidelines are frameworks developed to ensure the responsible development and deployment of AI, covering principles like fairness, transparency, accountability, and privacy.
55. **Q:** What is the role of AI in sustainability? **A:** AI can contribute to sustainability by optimizing resource use, reducing waste, improving energy efficiency, and enabling more effective environmental monitoring and management.

AI in Healthcare

56. **Q:** How is AI used in medical diagnostics? **A:** AI is used in medical diagnostics to analyze medical images, predict disease outbreaks, assist in diagnosis through pattern recognition, and provide personalized treatment recommendations.
57. **Q:** What is predictive analytics in healthcare? **A:** Predictive analytics in healthcare uses AI algorithms to analyze historical data to predict future events, such as disease progression, patient outcomes, and resource needs.
58. **Q:** How does AI assist in drug discovery? **A:** AI assists in drug discovery by analyzing biological data, predicting how different compounds interact with targets, and identifying potential drug candidates more efficiently.
59. **Q:** What are AI-powered wearable devices? **A:** AI-powered wearable devices are gadgets equipped with sensors and AI algorithms to monitor health metrics, such as heart rate, physical activity, and sleep patterns, providing insights and alerts for better health management.
60. **Q:** How can AI improve mental health care? **A:** AI can improve mental health care through applications like chatbots for initial screening and support, sentiment analysis in communications, and personalized therapy recommendations based on patient data.

AI in Finance

61. **Q:** What is algorithmic trading? **A:** Algorithmic trading involves using AI and algorithms to automatically execute trades based on pre-defined criteria, aiming to optimize trading strategies and improve market efficiency.
62. **Q:** How is AI used in fraud detection? **A:** AI is used in fraud detection by analyzing transaction data to identify unusual patterns and anomalies that may indicate fraudulent activity, enabling quicker and more accurate detection.
63. **Q:** What are robo-advisors? **A:** Robo-advisors are AI-powered platforms that provide automated financial planning and investment services, offering personalized advice and portfolio management.
64. **Q:** What is credit scoring with AI? **A:** Credit scoring with AI involves using machine learning algorithms to analyze various data points and assess an individual's creditworthiness more accurately than traditional methods.
65. **Q:** How does AI impact financial risk management? **A:** AI impacts financial risk management by providing advanced analytics to predict market trends, assess risk exposure, and develop strategies to mitigate potential financial losses.

AI in Education

66. **Q:** What is adaptive learning? **A:** Adaptive learning uses AI to personalize educational content and pacing based on individual students' learning needs, enhancing the learning experience and outcomes.
67. **Q:** How does AI assist in educational content creation? **A:** AI assists in educational content creation by generating customized learning materials, creating interactive content, and providing real-time feedback and assessments.
68. **Q:** What is an intelligent tutoring system (ITS)? **A:** An ITS is an AI-based system that provides personalized instruction and feedback to students, mimicking the support of a human tutor.
69. **Q:** How can AI improve administrative tasks in education? **A:** AI can improve administrative tasks by automating scheduling, grading, student enrollment, and data management, freeing up time for educators to focus on teaching.
70. **Q:** What are the ethical considerations of AI in education? **A:** Ethical considerations include ensuring data privacy, addressing biases in AI algorithms, maintaining transparency in AI decision-making, and providing equal access to AI-enhanced learning tools.

AI in Transportation

71. **Q:** What is an autonomous vehicle? **A:** An autonomous vehicle is a self-driving car that uses AI to navigate and operate without human intervention, relying on sensors, cameras, and machine learning algorithms.
72. **Q:** How is AI used in traffic management? **A:** AI is used in traffic management to analyze real-time traffic data, optimize signal timings, reduce congestion, and improve overall traffic flow.
73. **Q:** What is predictive maintenance in transportation? **A:** Predictive maintenance uses AI to analyze data from vehicles and infrastructure to predict failures and schedule maintenance proactively, reducing downtime and costs.
74. **Q:** How can AI enhance public transportation systems? **A:** AI can enhance public transportation by optimizing routes, improving scheduling, providing real-time updates, and analyzing passenger data to enhance service quality.
75. **Q:** What are the challenges of deploying AI in transportation? **A:** Challenges include ensuring safety and reliability, addressing legal and regulatory issues, managing public acceptance, and dealing with the ethical implications of autonomous decision-making.

AI in Manufacturing

76. **Q:** What is Industry 4.0? **A:** Industry 4.0 refers to the fourth industrial revolution, characterized by the integration of AI, IoT, robotics, and other advanced technologies in manufacturing.
77. **Q:** How does AI improve quality control in manufacturing? **A:** AI improves quality control by analyzing product data, detecting defects, predicting failures, and ensuring that products meet specified standards.
78. **Q:** What is predictive maintenance in manufacturing? **A:** Predictive maintenance in manufacturing uses AI to monitor equipment and predict when maintenance is needed, reducing downtime and extending machinery life.
79. **Q:** How does AI optimize supply chain management? **A:** AI optimizes supply chain management by predicting demand, optimizing inventory levels, improving logistics, and enhancing supplier management.
80. **Q:** What is the role of AI in robotic automation? **A:** AI enhances robotic automation by enabling robots to learn from data, adapt to new tasks, and work collaboratively with humans, improving efficiency and flexibility in manufacturing processes.

AI in Retail

81. **Q:** How is AI used in personalized marketing? **A:** AI is used in personalized marketing to analyze customer data and preferences, enabling targeted marketing campaigns, product recommendations, and personalized shopping experiences.
82. **Q:** What is dynamic pricing? **A:** Dynamic pricing involves using AI algorithms to adjust prices in real-time based on demand, competition, and other market factors, optimizing revenue.
83. **Q:** How does AI improve inventory management in retail? **A:** AI improves inventory management by predicting demand, optimizing stock levels, reducing overstock and stockouts, and streamlining supply chain operations.
84. **Q:** What are AI-powered chatbots in retail? **A:** AI-powered chatbots assist customers in real-time, providing product information, answering queries, processing orders, and enhancing customer service.
85. **Q:** How is AI used in visual search in retail? **A:** AI-powered visual search allows customers to upload images and find similar products, enhancing the shopping experience by making it easier to find desired items.

AI in Entertainment

86. **Q:** How does AI contribute to content recommendation? **A:** AI contributes to content recommendation by analyzing user behavior, preferences, and engagement to suggest relevant movies, music, articles, and other media.
87. **Q:** What is AI-generated content? **A:** AI-generated content involves using AI algorithms to create text, images, music, and videos, such as generating news articles, artwork, and music compositions.
88. **Q:** How is AI used in game development? **A:** AI is used in game development for creating intelligent NPCs (non-player characters), enhancing graphics, generating game levels, and personalizing player experiences.
89. **Q:** What is deepfake technology? **A:** Deepfake technology uses AI to create realistic but fake images, videos, or audio by superimposing existing media onto another, often used in entertainment and media production.
90. **Q:** What are virtual influencers? **A:** Virtual influencers are AI-generated personas that exist on social media, interacting with audiences, promoting products, and creating content like human influencers.

AI in Cybersecurity

91. **Q:** How does AI enhance threat detection in cybersecurity? **A:** AI enhances threat detection by analyzing network data, identifying patterns indicative of threats, and detecting anomalies that may indicate a cyber attack.
92. **Q:** What is an AI-based intrusion detection system (IDS)? **A:** An AI-based IDS monitors network traffic for suspicious activity, using machine learning to detect and respond to potential security breaches.
93. **Q:** How is AI used in phishing detection? **A:** AI is used in phishing detection by analyzing email content, URLs, and sender information to identify and block phishing attempts.
94. **Q:** What is the role of AI in endpoint security? **A:** AI enhances endpoint security by monitoring devices, detecting malicious activity, and providing real-time responses to protect against threats.
95. **Q:** How does AI help in incident response? **A:** AI assists in incident response by automating the detection, analysis, and remediation of security incidents, reducing response times and improving effectiveness.

AI in Agriculture

96. **Q:** How is AI used in precision farming? **A:** AI in precision farming involves using data and machine learning to optimize planting, fertilization, and irrigation, enhancing crop yield and resource efficiency.
97. **Q:** What is an AI-powered drone in agriculture? **A:** AI-powered drones are used for monitoring crop health, assessing soil conditions, mapping fields, and applying treatments, providing farmers with actionable insights.
98. **Q:** How does AI contribute to livestock management? **A:** AI contributes to livestock management by monitoring animal health, behavior, and productivity, enabling early detection of issues and optimizing feeding and breeding.
99. **Q:** What is the role of AI in weather prediction for agriculture? **A:** AI improves weather prediction by analyzing historical and real-time data, providing accurate forecasts to help farmers make informed decisions.
100. **Q:** How can AI help reduce food waste? **A:** AI can reduce food waste by optimizing supply chain logistics, improving inventory management, predicting demand, and ensuring better storage and distribution practices.

www.ingramcontent.com/pod-product-compliance
Lightning Source LLC
Chambersburg PA
CBHW082225220526
45470CB00010B/3312